A Griever's Handbook

Don't Cry Because It's Over

Smile Because it Happened

By Tom Butler

1st edition

ISBN: 978-0-359-05780-1

Printed in the United States of America

Introduction

This handbook is not written by a professional counselor, psychiatrist, psychologist, social worker, or a marriage or family therapist, but by one who has experienced the pain of losing his one and only love, my wife. I have read several self-help books on the grieving process and tried many things. I felt they have left out some things that can only be explained by one who has experienced it first-hand. It is my hope that by reading what I have experienced, that you can relate and see that these reactions are normal. Keeping in mind that everyone reacts differently, based on your life experiences.

Being the last born and the last one alive in my family, I feel I have experienced the gamut of most emotions of losing someone, except losing a child, which I pray nobody should have to endure. Hopefully, my stories will help you in someway and possibly give you some ideas about coping with the pain of your loss, which, never goes away.

When reading my experiences, keep in mind that I left home in Michigan for college in Colorado at the age of eighteen and settled in Colorado. Seeing my parents, brother and sister was very seldom often, as they had their families and careers to tend to as I did. Which partially explains how I coped with their passing.

Chapter One

The death of my family members

My first loss of a loved one was my mother, who died at the age of seventy. The loss of one who bore you, breast fed you and held you when you cried as a child is hard to take, especially if you are a youngster. It appears that the problems are different for girls and boys as each sex has their specific problems and connections to a mother or a father.

Professionals tell you if your father remarries, a stepmother can replace your real mom and vice versa. At least that is what they try to tell you, with the movies reinforcing that idea. But, having talked to friends that lost their birthright mother or father, this isn't how it really works. One never forgets the love for their real mother or father. I am told by many that a stepparent can be a really good friend, but they can never replace their birthright parent. I am sure some professionals would disagree with me about this.

In my case, my mother died in Michigan when I was married and had a family of my own in Colorado. My mother had suffered with heart problems and diabetes for many years and had one of her lower legs amputated. At this stage in life, I could only feel relief that her suffering had ended.

My second loss was my father-in-law living in Colorado. A very fine and upright man who had studied to become a priest at a young age, but fell in love with his wife, and they had two beautiful daughters. My father-in-law was a very good friend and gave me valuable advice throughout the years. His last few years were spent with very weak legs unable to walk. He was cared for at home, except for the last two weeks and passed away in the hospital of old age.

To lose a friend and confidant who accepted me as if I was his real son was a difficult loss for me. Living only 120 miles away, we spent many weekends at their house. I coped by praying for him and comforted my wife on the loss of her father.

My third loss was my mother-in-law. A very charming and wonderful woman who made me feel welcomed from day one. She was a wonderful cook and never spoke ill of anyone. She spent the last few months in a nursing home before she passed away. Again, I coped by praying for her and remembering our fond times.

My fourth loss was my father, who spent his last days at a nursing home in Michigan. I was fifty-two years old at the time and was very occupied with my family and career and although I felt remorse for his loss, it was easier to accept as he lived a long life.

If he would have died when I was young it would have been a different story. A child needs the advice and guidance of a father or mother. Hopefully, a child can find that special person to provide for what was lost by the death of their parent. Hopefully, they will never stop looking for that person. I was fortunate to have a father and mother-in-law who did an excellent job filling in for my birthright parents.

My one and only brother was eleven years older than me and he left home when I was seven years old for the military and Korean war, consequently we were never close. I tried to get closer to him when he returned from the military, but he quickly married. To be honest, I was closer to some of my friends, so his death did not impact me as much as the death of my sister.

My sister was six years older than me, but we were together as siblings until I was in high school. She was a help and influence on me and her death caused more sorrow and emptiness in my heart, even though we lived many miles apart.

So, as you can see a person's death and your reaction to it can be dependent on your relationship with that individual, your age, or your culture and religious beliefs, where you reside, and your interactions with that person.

This holds true for the loss of a pet. Adults and children cry and grieve over the loss of a dog or cat, as the pet may have been a constant companion or playmate. Even, soldiers and policemen shed tears when they lose their dog companions. Your loss is personal to you, don't feel ashamed or different if you don't react as people expect you to react.

Chapter Two

Facing the death of a spouse

The real reason behind this publication is to tell you about my loss of my only one love, Jeanne, and how I am coping after fifty-four years of marriage and two years of courtship. Jeanne suffered for several years due to cancer and the complications of the disease. I was her caretaker for those years and she lovingly called me her *'personal medic'*, a role I thoroughly embraced. I put my whole heart and soul into her care as I truly felt she was part of me. So much so, that I did not think God would take her away that fateful night.

Her last two weeks were at home. Even though we talked about death and her wishes, I was the eternal optimist thinking she would get better. I was in denial. The last night she was weak and ate very little supper. Thinking she was just tired, I decided to sleep in a chair by her bed in case she would need something, but I became uncomfortable at 4:30 in the morning. I arose from the chair and found her arms out of the covers and cold. Not wanting to disturb her sleep I put her sweater over her arms and not opening her eyes, she smiled. I went into my bed for about an hour and returned to see if she needed anything and she was gone. God came like a thief in the night and took her soul.

Her death just didn't seem real. The first few weeks it was difficult for me to sleep at night and I experienced anxiety and panic at times. My daughter and grand daughter thought a trip away from home would help me, but I panicked the first night out and felt I had to return home. Your children can be a great help in helping to cope with your loss and they have been for me. But, eventually, they need to attend to their lives and family.

I tried attending meetings where others have recently lost their loved ones, but it didn't seem to help me. Maybe for you it may help. It is worth a try if you haven't experienced it yet.

I kept going over in my mind what I or the doctors could have done differently. I experienced anger that the doctors didn't or couldn't do more to help her. For a while I was mad at God for taking her away from me. Later, I thanked God for the time she was with me. I read one metaphor that stated; *'When you pick flowers in a garden don't you pick the most beautiful ones first? Well, God does the same thing.'*

At this point, about six months after her death, I made up my mind that I needed to get my health in better shape as doctors can only do so much for you and having seen how understaffed hospitals are, I wanted no part of it. I used the Mayo Clinic diet and dropped forty pounds and started going to the community recreation center to work out. This has helped me mentally and allowed me to decrease some medications. I found that when you feel good physically it's easier to cope emotionally.

During the last three years I am still working on cleaning, updating and discarding things accumulated over fifty years of living in one house. This was one of Jeanne's wishes that I keep the house up as she loved our home. I still keep the yard and flowers the same as if she was here. Even though she is physically gone, I believe she is here spiritually even now as I write this.

Some people ask me, "Why are you still living in that house all alone?" Some people move away when they lose someone close to them. They think the pain will go away if you get away from it. My neighbors lost a son in the Vietnam war and this is what they did as they couldn't bare to walk in his bedroom. This only made it worse for them in the long run. You can't escape the pain. Why move and leave beautiful memories, unless you can't keep up the house.

I have found for real healing it is necessary to face it and actively deal with the loss, by doing certain things to cope. After the first year, I started to go back to our roots and visited the college where we first met and other familiar places, even returning to Michigan where I grew up to get my bearings in life again and to remind myself of the goals and purpose of my life.

When I returned home to Colorado, I realized I needed to start being thankful for the years I did have with Jeanne and not dwell on what I don't have. It may sound silly to some, but I proceeded to put together a picture frame of twenty-four photos showing her at different ages of her life, writing a book about her and her Slovenian culture, as well as a book about our life together before our two girls were born. I vowed to celebrate her life and keep her memory alive by her pictures throughout the house. I even have a picture of her on my center console of my car as a reminder she is with me always. I planted two rose bushes, one purple as that was her favorite color and one white for her purity, by my front door as a memorial to her. One could plant a tree as well as other memorials.

After three years of keeping busy, I am coping, but I still have set backs at times. It is never easy to live alone, and her loss has left me emotional. Now when I see a movie or a television program where someone dies, or it is an emotional moment tears begin to form.

The one thing that helps my mood when I start getting down or bored is to listen to music that we enjoyed together. It must be upbeat music though, as sad songs can bring tears to your eyes. I also try to keep and continue what we did as a couple and cook (Fortunately I can cook) In other words, keeping things the same and follow the same routines. This helps me to not feel her loss as much.

You will experience ups and downs. The downs were longer in the beginning, but are shorter now, three years later. Special events and holidays can be downers, but lately, I say to myself, "What would Jeanne do, what would she cook or how would she decorate?" I try to keep traditions alive, which helps me. Remember, there is no typical response to loss as every loss is not typical, except to you.

It was suggested to me that I should find someone new. So, I signed up for the Catholic dating service. I corresponded with several. But, this is complicated at my age as people have families and other interests. I found it hard to find something in common with most and gave up on the idea, which was not my idea in the first place.

Match making may work for you, but not for me. My cousin lost his love of his life and he remarried, not for love, but as he said, "For companionship". I am now seventy-six years old and healthy, set in my ways, and if someone wanted to change the way things are done or how Jeanne has something, I would resent that person for it as I cling to tradition and her memory. Don't tell me to move on or forget her as she was a part of me and in my soul.

Another thing that has helped me and may help you too and that is to pursue your interests that maybe you couldn't do before, such as a hobby or getting back to activities that bring you joy and satisfaction. For me I enjoy writing and have written a few self-published books through Lulu.com. Also, home projects I couldn't get to before and in the winter spending my idle time on 1000-piece puzzles. The point is keeping busy helps to not dwell on your loss.

If you have a religious faith it can be important to your healing by continuing your religious practices, and religious reading. But, be forewarned attending religious services can bring out your emotions and tears as it brings back memories of what you did together.

Lastly, if you cannot seem to cope and nothing helps don't be ashamed to go for professional help and guidance.

There are numerous quotes available about losing a loved one available on the internet and elsewhere. These have helped me to express my grief. I have included some of these on the following pages. Excuse my use of some minions, I find them amusing and uplifting.

ON THE ANNIVERSARY OF THE

Day You Went Away

Today's the anniversary
Of the day that I lost you,
And for a time it felt as though
My life had ended too.

But loss has taught me many things
And now I face each day,
With hope and happy memories
To help me on my way.

And though I'm full of sadness
That you're no longer here,
Your influence still guides me
And I still feel you near.

What we shared will never die
It lives within my heart,
Bringing strength and comfort
While we are apart.

Sometimes all you can do is smile. Move on with your day, hold back the tears and pretend you're okay.

I hide my tears when i say your name. But the pain in my heart is still the same. Though i smile & seem carefree. Theres no one who misses you more than me x

The Day God Took You Home

A million times
I've needed you
A million times I've cried,
If love alone
Could have saved you
you never would have died.
In life I loved you dearly,
In death I love you still.
In my heart you hold a place,
No one else can ever fill.
It broke my heart to lose you,
But you didn't go alone
Part of me went with you,
The day God took you home.

As long as I live
You will live,

As long as I live
You will be remembered,

As long as I live
You will be loved.

We talk about them because we're proud. We talk about them, because they deserve to be remembered. We talk about them, because even though they are not physically with us, they are never far from our mind. We talk about them, because they are part of us, a part that we could never ignore or disown. We talk about them because we love them still and always will. Forever. Nothing will ever change that.

DO NOT REGRET
GROWING OLDER.

IT IS A PRIVILEGE
DENIED TO MANY

There are moments in life when you wish you could bring someone down from heaven. To spend the day with them just one more time, give them one more hug, kiss them goodbye or hear their voice again. One more chance to say I Love You!

Time doesn't heal anything... It just teaches us how to live with THE PAIN.

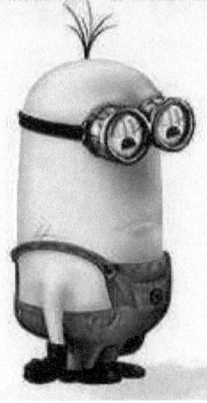

In Memory of all my family
and friends who have
passed away.

I miss you,
I think about
you and
I will never
forget you.
I love you, always.

Chapter Three

Some Other Suggestions

When you lose someone you love, I feel you must take it one day at a time. For me, grief has been an opportunity to redefine myself and to look for new meaning and vision for the remaining years of my life. Life is so uncertain. You never know if God is just around the next corner waiting to take you home.

I have talked to many friends and acquaintances who have lost their mate. There is no quick fix. You must decide what is right for you. For me, the first thing I did was to keep busy cleaning the house and respecting my wife's last wishes. One request was to clean and throw all her clothes away and not give them to charity. It may sound heartless to you, but she said she did not want someone to wear her clothes and I respected that.

Some professionals will tell you not to dwell on the past and as soon as possible to focus on the present. For me it has been possible to do both. How can one forget the beautiful years together and cherish that memory and at the same time focus on the present. They say you should be able to talk and think about your loved one without emotional pain, but you just learn to live with pain. Pain never goes away.

Remember, as much as you go over events of your loss and what you may or could have done to prevent it, we can't do anything about what has happened. We just must eventually except what has happened and focus on our future. God would not want us to give up on life or ourselves. God has another plan for you and nobody knows what the reasons are. Very possibly, the work on you and your soul is not complete.

One thing that has helped me is to self-educate myself about grief and healing. The first place I looked was to my friends who have lost their mates in life. Find out from them how and what they have and are doing to cope with grief. Also, hospitals have bereavement programs that you can tap into. Albeit, not all will pertain to you, which I found out when I attended a bereavement program. Everyone in the group has a different perspective of their loss. Do what is right for you.

Search the library and book stores for books on grieving and if you have a computer, the internet has numerous articles about grieving and coping. They say we should heal, but a part of you is gone, one can only learn to cope with the situation. Ask yourself, "*What would my mate want me to do?*" Making the right choices affects how we cope with our loss. Choices dictate the quality of our lives and our health and you always have a choice. Don't despair, keep telling yourself, "*I am going to make it through this!*"

Even though your loved one is gone physically, they are in your heart, a piece of you. I can not help but feel my wife is always with me spiritually and every morning I say good morning to her smiling picture. At night I tell her good night and that I love her. Then I say a prayer for her soul.

Prayer has been an integral part of our life. I know this is not true for some of you. To explain, during my youth my family did not pray or go to church. I felt something was missing in my life and started to pray and attend church on my own when a teenager. Where I grew up was largely a protestant community. However, I found the churches lacking and converted to Catholicism when I was in college. This being said, my wife was educated by the Benedictine Sisters so consequently prayer was a big part of our lives. Prayer has helped me to express my feelings and gain comfort in spiritual readings.

Luckily, in my case, my wife and I had time to talk about her death and wishes. She knew she was reaching the end, but I never gave up hope and didn't see it coming when it did. Besides telling me her wishes and where and how her body would be, I told her that I didn't know how I could survive without her. She gave me words of encouragement as she did throughout our marriage and told me I will do just fine. Her words of encouragement helped to give me the confidence to go on and make the right choices. After all, one wouldn't want to disappoint the one they love, and I am sure you wouldn't want to either.

Do not be afraid. At first, I spent a few restless nights and still do occasionally. I would wake up and suddenly feel very anxious and start to panic. You just can't relax and go to sleep. For me, I would get up, turn on the lights, listen to music, watch Television, play a computer game, read a book, pray or anything that will help me to calm down. It is in times of inactions that I would start to panic. But, by talking to oneself and doing something to occupy your mind you can get through the panic attack. If you need professional help don't be afraid to go for it.

Remember, grief has many ups and downs. Some days are worse for me than others. I've read that grief is like an ocean wave with its highs and lows. This is normal I am told. When you are low this is the time to get up and get moving and remember a low day will pass. You just need to work at it and do something, such as talking to someone or finding something to do, like I am right now and that is writing this book, which gives me comfort knowing that just maybe this book will help you.

One thing that has helped me to cope with my loss is to connect with old friends from high school and college. I know there are certain times of the year that I'll be less busy at home, so I plan vacations and trips that I was not able to do before. I love to drive and listen to music.

I must tell you that in the first few months I was using words such as "could've, should've, would've" and don't be surprised if you do too. Let go of these negative thoughts and don't down grade yourself. Ask yourself, "Did I do what I thought I should do at the time?" Of course, you did. Don't lay a guilt trip on yourself. However, I did for a short time and only by talking with someone about it did I see what I was doing. Try not to fall into this trap.

I mentioned special events and holidays before but try to plan these events. I celebrate the holidays with my daughters and plan an evening out to celebrate my deceased birthday and our anniversary. My daughter bakes a special cake that my wife always wanted on her birthday. Carrying on traditions are I feel a great help in coping. Why would you want to drop everything? This would only make you feel worse. A friend of mine has a cabin in northern Michigan that he and his wife always went to in the summer. He still carries on as if she was with him at the cabin as it brings many good memories back to him. For me it is taking my daughter and grand daughter to the state fair which was the event of our first date and to see some of the old haunts where we courted. Don't let good memories die.

Going to the graveyard can work either way for you. I go and sit by her place in the mausoleum to pray and look at the spot where I'll be right next to her, and to change the artificial flowers for the change in seasons.

These visits help me accept her death and gives me great satisfaction knowing I have a place by her side.

My parents, brother and sister are buried 1200 miles away in Michigan, but when I make it back for a visit I always try to visit their gravesites. My wife's family are buried 3 hours drive from here and regrettably I don't make a visit that often. The reason for this is that it causes a down day as I miss my wife, all the deceased family, and relatives who were so good to me.

I know I am still learning how to cope, but I see myself making progress. It bothers me that I shed tears when something emotional occurs in a movie as I feel embarrassed. I know this is normal, but it is at times hard to control. I have adjusted to church most of the time as some events or songs will just trigger my emotions. Consequently, I don't always go as often to church as I used to. This is just another way for me to cope with my loss. Always, do whatever works for you.

One thing in my readings that I didn't come across was the role of a pet. My wife and I have a dog which we obtained four years before her death. I was left with our dog, Princess. A pet can be a comfort as I talk to Princess. No, I am not crazy! Princess will sit and look at me with her brown eyes as if she understands. One evening shortly after Jeanne's passing on, Princess was in the house and sat down in front of the chair where Jeanne always sat and just stared at the empty chair for several seconds, which gave me goosebumps. One can only imagine what was in the mind of Princess. A pet can help if you are so inclined.

I know I will eventually die, as death seems to be the only certain thing in life. Being left alone and the last one in a family is rather daunting. Being a history buff, I can only wonder how our ancestors who came through all the deaths during the Revolutionary War, Civil War, settling of the West, and World wars came through it all?

I came across a poem/prayer which I feel says it all.

Time like an ever-rolling stream

Bears all its sons away

They fly forgotten, as a dream

Dies at the opening day

O God, our help in ages past,

Our hope for years to come,

Be thou our guard while troubles last,

And our eternal home. Amen

One more thing I remember hearing years ago, which easily could be spoken by God, "I may have promised you a rose garden, but I didn't say there wouldn't be any thorns.

I realize now that loss and coping is a lifelong process, something you rarely think about when you are young. It is not an option, nor can it be avoided. Everyone will experience it. It is our duty to survive losses. What if our early settlers had given up with their losses, we wouldn't be here today.

One and the most important thing to remember is that each of us handles the loss of a loved one differently. There is no set time limit to grieve. When I asked a friend (who lost his wife) how he was doing, he always said I miss my wife and he said this until he passed away eight years after his wife. I still miss my wife and I know I always will, until I lay besides her at the mausoleum.

I wish you the best in coping with your loss. It is my opinion that one never heals but learns to live with the pain. I am reminded of a story of a man who as a young boy lost all his family to an American Indian attack and he himself was severely injured and left for dead. He was the only survivor, but he learned to cope and was quoted as saying he missed his family until the day of his death.

I would like to recommend a song by Rod Stewart for you to listen to and that is the song "Sailing". I have shortened the lyrics as follows as lyrics are duplicated in places.

I am sailing home again "cross the sea. I am sailing stormy waters to be near you, to be free. I am flying like a bird "cross the sky. I am flying passing high clouds to be with you to be free. Can you hear me, through the dark night, far-away? I am dying, forever crying to be with you, who can say. We are sailing, home again "cross the sea, we are sailing stormy waters to be near you to be free. Oh Lord, to be near you, to be free.

Rod Stewart has several videos on You Tube of this song, but there is one, which is religiously inspiring. I am unable to replicate the title on the computer because of the symbols, but it is "a beamed note, heart, quaver/eighth note, word Sailing, a beamed note, heart, quaver/eighth note, By Rod Stewart – lyrics"

I recall this from some of my readings and for me it says it all.

Attitude creates reality. How you view a situation can have an enormous impact on how you live. Some people see losses as absolute devastations, whereas others view them as opportunities. At the end of the day, the choice is really up to you.

Best wishes for your journey.

About the Author

Tom grew up in southern Michigan near the Indiana/Ohio border in a rural farming community. He left Michigan in 1960, attended college in Pueblo, Colorado where he met his wife. They were married in 1963 and eventually resided in the Denver, Colorado area where they had two daughters. Tom worked for what is now called Xcel Energy for thirty-six years while at the same time going to night school to obtain his master's degree, retiring from Xcel Energy in 2002. Tom lost his wife, Jeanne, after being together fifty-five years. Tom remains in the same home they have lived in for fifty-one years.

Tom has written several self-published books through Lulu.com under the name of Tom Butler and T. Lee Butler.

Notes